Roll Over

There were eight in the bed
and the little one said...

Roll over, roll over.

So they all rolled over
and one fell out.

So they all rolled over
and one fell out.

There were six in the bed
and the little one said...

"Roll over, roll over."

So they all rolled over
and one fell out.

So they all rolled over
and one fell out.

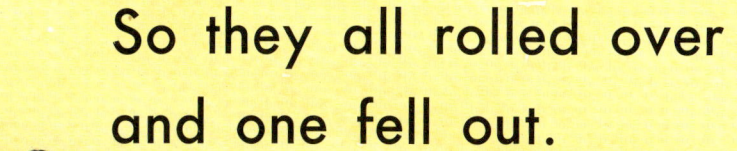

There were four in the bed and the little one said...

Roll over, roll over.

So they all rolled over and one fell out.

There were three in the bed
and the little one said...

So they all rolled over and one fell out.

So they all rolled over and one fell out.